Spreadsheet Skills for Budgeting

Sue Nugus

Viva Books Private Limited
New Delhi • Mumbai • Chennai • Kolkata

First South Asian Edition 2002

VIVA BOOKS PRIVATE LIMITED

- 4262/3 Ansari Road, Daryaganj, New Delhi 110 002
  e-mail : viva@mantraonline.com
- 214 New Apollo Industrial Estate, 2nd Floor, Mogra Lane, Andheri (E), Mumbai 400 069
  e-mail : vivabooks@mantraonline.com
- 7 Aziz Mulk, Seventh Street, Thousand Lights, Chennai 600 006
  e-mail : vivachennai@mantraonline.com
- 6-A, Rifle Range Road, Kolkata 700 019
  e-mail : vivakolkata@mantraonline.com

Visit us at **www.vivagroupindia.com**

Published by Arrangement with
The Chartered Institute of Management Accountants
26 Chapter Street
London SW1P 4NP
UK.

ISBN : 81-7649-318-X

Rs. 100

Published by Vinod Vasishtha for Viva Books Private Limited,
4262/3 Ansari Road, Daryaganj, New Delhi 110 002
Printed at Raj Press, R-3 Inderpuri, New Delhi - 110012

Contents

CHAPTER 4
Working with Spreadsheets 35

CHAPTER 5
Working with Other Applications 53

Chapter 1

Introduction to Budgetary Control

A budget is a detailed estimate of future transactions. It can be expressed in terms of physical quantities, money, or both. The essence of a budget is that it is a target set for management to achieve or surpass. Thus a budget is always associated with a specific departmental responsibility point or centre within the firm. This might be a division that has a sales budget, a factory with a capital budget, or an individual with an expense budget. Whatever the case, there will normally be an individual responsible for achieving the budget.

SCOPE OF BUDGETING

Budgetary control is not limited to commercial and industrial firms attempting to produce a profit. The procedures involved are equally applicable to *not-for-profit* organisations such as government departments, universities and charities.

All aspects of the business or organisation can be budgeted. There might be *income and expenditure* budgets, *cash* budgets, *capital* budgets, *research and development* budgets, to mention only a few examples. Budgets can be classified as *master* budgets, *departmental* budgets or *functional* budgets. Whatever level or degree of detail, a budget is useless if it does not focus on a point of responsibility.

Budgeting is a management function that incorporates:

1. setting objectives;
2. establishing detailed financial estimates;
3. delegating specific responsibility;
4. monitoring performance;
5. reacting to expectations.

BENEFITS OF BUDGETING

The benefits of budgetary control can usefully be classified in the following way:

1. a budget forces management to express in figures its future intentions;
2. it provides a yardstick by which individuals or groups can be measured and rewarded;
3. it allows some responsibility and authority to be decentralised without loss of information required by management for control purposes;
4. budgeting provides a mechanism to control in detail the revenue, costs, cash and capital expenditure of the firm;
5. it facilitates an atmosphere of cost-consciousness;
6. it helps to ensure that return on investment is optimised.

DIFFERENT APPROACHES TO BUDGETING

There are various approaches to the preparation of a budgeting system, but two popular methods are the *traditional approach* and the *zero-based budgeting approach*.

With the traditional approach some firms simply recompile last year's or the previous period's figures, adjusted for expected growth or for inflation. This approach to formulating a budget relies on the notion that all the business variables will remain more or less the same in relationship to one another from one period to the next. For this type of budget, after preparing an initial set of figures, a minimal amount of preparation is required.

Some firms adopt the view that the most important aspect of budgetary control lies in the fact that the creation of budgets should impose on the firm a *strict regime of thinking through* what the firm is doing and where it is going. This approach has been popularised under the title of zero-based budgeting (ZBB) and assumes that it is necessary to start the budgeting process from scratch each time. The main advantage of this approach is that is ensures a rethink of the basic business assumptions on which the firm relies. With a ZBB system, each functional section in the business will plan in detail all revenue, expenditure and capital items, and these items will be ranked in order of importance to the firm.

An outcome from a ZBB system that is not the case with the traditional approach is that management are forced to prove the need for each item of expenditure in the budget. It is not good enough to say that the promotion account had a particular amount in it last year and that this figure should be increased by *x* per cent for inflation. Clearly it is more expensive to operate a ZBB system than a traditional system, and therefore a cost-benefit study is appropriate before embarking on a ZBB.

The term ZBB is generally associated with the budgeting of indirect costs. It is therefore used extensively in central service departments, marketing and distribution, and research and development. ZBB is not considered to be directly relevant to the manufacturing process, as detailed expenditure in this area is usually automatically accounted for on a variable or direct basis.

BUDGET PREPARATION

The procedure and operation of any budgetary control system is clearly specific to each individual organisation and is a function of management style and corporate culture. However, there are general guidelines that are useful to bear in mind.

Establishing the firm's objectives

This usually involves a lengthy process of analysing the firm's strengths and weaknesses and matching these to the opportunities in the environment in which the firm functions. This is sometimes referred to as strategic planning. This is a senior management activity which is an ongoing process coming to a focal point at budget time. A top-down approach is normally dominant here.

Forecasting the key business variables

Before any figures can be derived an activity forecast must be established. In many organisations this means that a sales forecast must be produced, which can be a lengthy and difficult process. It is important to ensure that a broad spectrum of people is involved and committed to the sales forecast. Therefore both top-down and bottom-up approaches are appropriate here.

Calculating physical estimates

The number of people, the scale of equipment and the volumes of raw materials required must be established. This is usually a bottom-up procedure.

Making detailed costings of each responsibility centre
This requires the involvement of a wide variety of staff and can lead to a considerable amount of negotiation. Thus both top-down and bottom-up approaches are required.

These activities are best conducted in a cyclical fashion, with feedback being sent up and down the organisation at various times, representing how different groups feel about the suggestions being made. Thus the amount of time required to produce a budget can be substantial.

SPREADSHEETS FOR BUDGETS

A spreadsheet can be used to support both the traditional approach to budgeting and the zero-based approach.

With the traditional approach, having initially designed and developed a plan with care, continuous use of the system is largely a case of changing the input data. Template techniques shown in this book are invaluable in this situation.

Templates can also form the basis of zero-based budgets as, even when starting from scratch, an outline of the requirements for the budget is known and a template can form the basis of the new budget.

SUMMARY

Budgeting is an essential part of modern management and is regularly performed in most organisations. It is as much a management philosophy and technique as an approach to financial accounting.

The spreadsheet is a particularly powerful tool in the development of budgets. It is also useful for the production of reports such as budget–actual–variance, year-to-date totals and consolidated results.

■ Chapter 2

Designing and Creating a Budgetary Control System

PREPLANNING

A budgetary control system will require a number of different modules, and precisely what these are will differ from organisation to organisation and from department to department. However, a typical situation might be the requirement for departmental budgets, actuals, variance and year-to-date reports. Selected data from these reports is then likely to be required at corporate level to form part of the overall aggregated reports for the organisation.

For anything other than the simplest spreadsheet application there are clear key stages to model development that should be strictly adhered to. Figure 2.1 illustrates these.

Figure 2.1 Stages in the spreadsheet development process

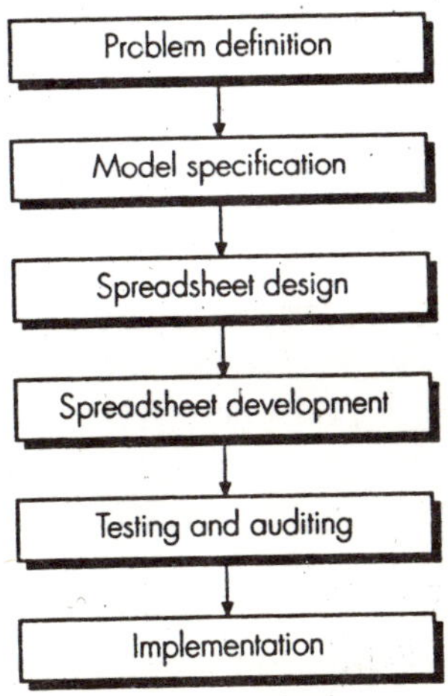

Problem definition

Before beginning to enter data and formulae into the spreadsheet it is important to think carefully about the problem that is to be solved by the creation of the spreadsheet system. This will often involve talking to a number of people who might need to extract information from the system when it is complete. It is much more difficult to change the format of a plan after it has been committed to the spreadsheet. At this stage the level of detail required in the model should be established. There are many examples of spreadsheet systems that include detailed calculations which are irrelevant to the analysis of the problem or which are never reported on or used by anyone working with the system.

Model specification

At this stage the assumptions that will be made should be considered. In addition, the overall format of the system – in terms of what information will be kept on what sheet, and what data will be stored in separate files – should be decided and agreed by all who have a vested interest in the system.

Spreadsheet design

The detailed breakdown of how the system is to be laid out should be considered here. This includes how data input forms will be used, how much of the descriptive information can be repeated for different parts of the system, how much documentation will be included in the system, etc.

Spreadsheet development

This is the stage at which the actual building of the logic required for the system takes place. All too often, spreadsheet developers pay little or no attention to the preceding stages and jump into spreadsheet development straightaway. The results of this approach invariably lead to unnecessarily complex models that take longer than necessary to develop; assumptions are made that were not part of the original brief, and in some cases the result can be an inappropriate system for others to work with.

Testing

Even with thorough preplanning and careful spreadsheet development it is important to test all sections of a system. This involves entering several sets of data and exhaustively checking the logic. If historical data with known results is available this can be useful for testing purposes.

Implementation

The effort required for implementation will vary, depending on the system being developed, its complexity, the number of individuals who will use the system and whether training or ongoing assistance is required. However, it is worth noting that even if a system is seen as a single-user application, individuals do change jobs and therefore it is wise to assume that someone other than the developer might have to use or amend the spreadsheet at some stage.

A WORKED EXAMPLE

The example that will be used throughout this book is a quarterly budgetary control system for a fictitious toy manufacturing company called Techno-Toy Ltd. Techno-Toy has three factories in the United Kingdom. These are referred to as Techno-Leeds, Techno-Bristol and Techno-London. The London factory is also the location for the head office, and the financial manager at head office has been asked to design a budgeting system. The system requires each regional factory to complete a template of budgeted data every quarter that is then aggregated into a corporate budget at head office. Each region is also required to prepare periodic variance and year-to-date reports, and thus they need to be able to enter actual data as it becomes available on a quarterly basis in order to prepare these reports.

SMALL IS BEAUTIFUL

When designing any spreadsheet system it is important to spend time deciding how it can be broken down into manageable sections. In terms of the spreadsheet this means looking at what information should be placed on separate sheets within a single file, and what information should be stored on separate files and then be accessed, when required, using file links, or other spreadsheet consolidation features.

For practical purposes in this book only a small amount of sample data has been used. However, the principles discussed here apply to most systems, whether they be a large number of periods and a large number of line items, or whether it is a summary situation.

Figure 2.2 is a plan of the different sections that comprise the Techno-Toy budgetary control system.

Figure 2.2: Plan of the overall budgetary control system for Techno-Toy Ltd

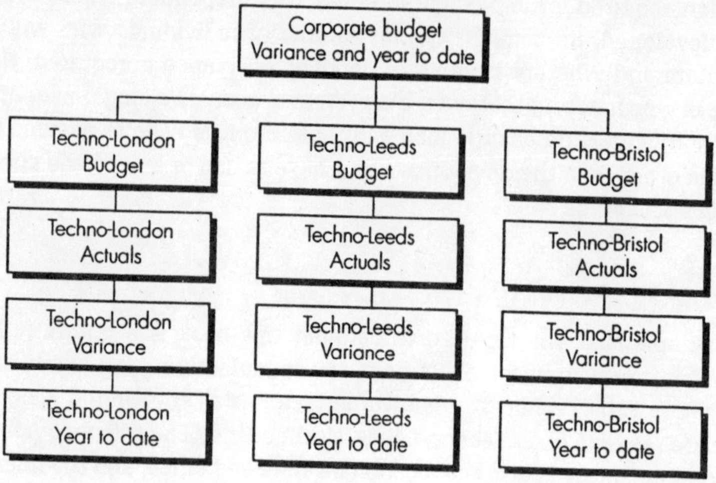

Each regional department will have a copy of the same system comprising four files, which for the purposes of this exercise will be called *Budget*, *Actual*, *Variance* and *YTD*. These files will be developed initially for one region with historical data so that the logic can be fully tested and audited. The files will then be made into templates for the other regions to use.

A template is a file that contains all the logic or formulae, but no data. It is saved on disk with a special extension – .XLT in the case of Excel and WKT in the case of 1–2–3. Template files are difficult to overwrite and help to ensure that the user always enters a new set of data into a blank file.

It is assumed for the purpose of this book that although the input data will be different for the different regions, the underlying logic of the budget and actual files is the same.

DEVELOPING THE MASTER BUDGET FILE

The assumptions for the master budget file which will be developed initially for the London factory of Techno-Toy is as follows:

- sales commence at 6,250 and increase at 1 per cent per quarter;
- unit price is £25 and remains constant;
- direct costs are 35 per cent of turnover;

overhead costs commence at £21,000 and increase at 1 per cent per quarter.

It is important to spend time itemising the assumptions for any plan into a list before entering any information into the spreadsheet.

The next step is to decide on the layout of this information on the spreadsheet. It is important to keep all data input separate from the logic of a plan as this facilitates easier updating and auditing of the plan. Therefore two sheets will be used for the master budget file. The first sheet will be called *Budget* and will contain all the logic and formulae, and the second sheet will be called *Input* into which all the input will be entered. Figure 2.3 is a plan of the worksheets that will be used for the master budget file.

Figure 2.3: Plan of the worksheets for the master budget file

Summar y budget file

- Sales
- Unit price
- Revenue
- Direct costs
- Gross profit
- Overhead costs
- Net profit

Budgetsheet

Input form

- Sales and sales growth
- Unit price and growth
- Direct costs as a percentage
- Overhead costs and growth

Inputsheet

Figures 2.4 and 2.5 show the completed model and the input form, using the data described in the assumptions above.

The cells into which data is to be entered have been shaded to make them clear. Once the system is complete and has been fully tested, both sheets of this file can be protected and only those cells into which data can be entered should be left unprotected.

When developing a multi-sheet plan such as this it is recommended that you enter the headings and row descriptions on all sheets first. In this way, when the formulae are being entered it is clear what cell references are required and the mouse can be used to point to cells as formulae are constructed.

Figure 2.4 Master budget with data

	A	B	C	D	E	F
1			**Techno-Toy Ltd**			
2			*Summary Budget for 19xx*			
3		**Qtr1**	**Qtr2**	**Qtr3**	**Qtr4**	**Total**
4	**Sales**	6250	6313	6376	6439	25378
5	**Unit Price**	25.00	25.00	25.00	25.00	
6	**Revenue**	**156250**	**157813**	**159391**	**160985**	**634438**
7						
8	**Direct Costs**	70313	71016	71726	72443	285497
9						
10	**Gross Profit**	**85938**	**86797**	**87665**	**88541**	**348941**
11						
12	**Overheads**	21000	21210	21422	21636	85268
13						
14	**Net Profit**	**64938**	**65587**	**66243**	**66905**	**263672**

Budgets / Input / Sheet3 / Sheet4 / Sheet5 / Sheet6 / Sheet7 / She

Notice in cell C4 of the *Budget* sheet (Figure 2.6) the use of an absolute reference to Cell C5 of the *Input* sheet by preceding the row and column reference with a dollar sign, $C$4. This fixes the reference to the cell so that when the formula is extrapolated for the remaining quarters the reference to that cell remains the same. This technique has been used wherever data from the *Input* sheet has been referenced.

Having checked the logic this file can be saved with the name BUDGET.

Figure 2.5 Input form for master budget with data

	A	B	C	D	E
1	Budget input form				
2					
3		Opening	Growth	Opening	
4		Value	Rate	Proportion	
5	Sales	6250	1.00%		
6	Unit Price	25	0.00%		
7					
8	Direct Costs			45.00%	of turnover
9	Overhead Costs	21000	1.00%		
10					
11					
12					
13					
14					
15					
16					
17					
18					
19					
20					
21					
22					
23					
24					

Budgets | Input | Sheet3 | Sheet4 | Sheet5 | Sheet6 | Sheet7

Figure 2.6 shows the logic that has been used for the *Budget* sheet.

Figure 2.6 Logic for the *Budget* sheet

	A	B	C	D	E	F
1				Techno-Toy Ltd		
2				*Summary Budget for 19xx*		
3		Qtr1	Qtr2	Qtr3	Qtr4	Total
4	Sales	=Input!B5	=B4*(1+Input!$C$5)	=C4*(1+Input!$C$5)	=D4*(1+Input!$C$5)	=SUM(B4:E4)
5	Unit Price	=Input!B6	=B5*(1+Input!$C$6)	=C5*(1+Input!$C$6)	=D5*(1+Input!$C$6)	
6	Revenue	=B4*B5	=C4*C5	=D4*D5	=E4*E5	=SUM(B6:E6)
7						
8	Direct Costs	=B6*Input!$D$8	=C6*Input!$D$8	=D6*Input!$D$8	=E6*Input!$D$8	=SUM(B8:E8)
9						
10	Gross Profit	=B6-B8	=C6-C8	=D6-D8	=E6-E8	=SUM(B10:E10)
11						
12	Overheads	=Input!B9	=B12*(1+Input!$C$9)	=C12*(1+Input!$C$9)	=D12*(1+Input!$C$9)	=SUM(B12:E12)
13						
14	Net Profit	=B10-B12	=C10-C12	=D10-D12	=E10-E12	=SUM(B14:E14)
15						

CREATING A TEMPLATE

In order to use this file for different departments and with different data, the existing data can be removed and the file can then be stored on the disk as a template file. Because the master budget file has been created using a separate data input form, all that is required to convert this file into a template is to remove the data on the *Input* sheet. Figures 2.7 and 2.8 show the BUDGET file after removing the data.

Removing data from a spreadsheet plan is a useful auditing technique. If the relationships have been properly constructed there should be only zeros, or possibly division by zero errors, displayed. If the spreadsheet is displaying values after removing the input data this indicates that a formula might have been overwritten or that input data has been embedded into formulae as opposed to being entered separately.

Figure 2.7 Budget file without data

	A	B	C	D	E	F
1			**Techno-Toy London Ltd**			
2			***Summary Budget for 19XX***			
3		**Qtr1**	**Qtr2**	**Qtr3**	**Qtr4**	**Total**
4	**Sales**	0	0	0	0	0
5	**Unit Price**	0.00	0.00	0.00	0.00	
6	**Revenue**	**0**	**0**	**0**	**0**	**0**
7						
8	**Direct Costs**	0	0	0	0	0
9						
10	**Gross Profit**	**0**	**0**	**0**	**0**	**0**
11						
12	**Overheads**	0	0	0	0	0
13						
14	**Net Profit**	**0**	**0**	**0**	**0**	**0**
15						

Figure 2.8 Input form without data

	A	B	C	D	E
1	Budget input form				
2					
3		Opening	Growth	Opening	
4		Value	Rate	Proportion	
5	Sales				
6	Unit Price				
7					
8	Direct Costs				of turnover
9	Overhead Costs				
10					
11					

Both Excel and 1–2–3 have a feature that allows a spreadsheet to be saved as a template file. It will have an extension of .XLT in the case of Excel and .WKT in the case of 1–2–3.

To save the BUDGET file as a template select **File Save As** and type in a filename. In this example the name BUDTEMP is suggested. In the Save as type box select Template (*.xlt) for Excel and SmartMaster (wt4) for 1–2–3. Close the file after saving.

To use the template, select **File New** as opposed to **File Open**.

In Excel all template files are stored in a common directory by default, although this can be changed if necessary. Therefore on selecting **File New** the BUDTEMP file will be displayed as an available template.

In 1–2–3 templates are stored in the current directory and therefore on selecting **File New** the .WKT file is likely to be displayed. If a required template is in a different directory select **Browse** and then choose the appropriate directory.

In either case once the template file has been selected, a copy of the file is opened, leaving the original template safely on the disk. After entering data into the file, selecting File Save will offer the name BUDTEMP1.XLS in Excel and FILE0001.WK4 in 1–2–3. Of course, these names can be overwritten with something more appropriate, but it ensures that an existing file will not be overwritten and also ensures that the file will be saved as a worksheet file as opposed to a template file.

CREATING THE ACTUALS FILE

Figure 2.9 Actuals file with sample data for first quarter

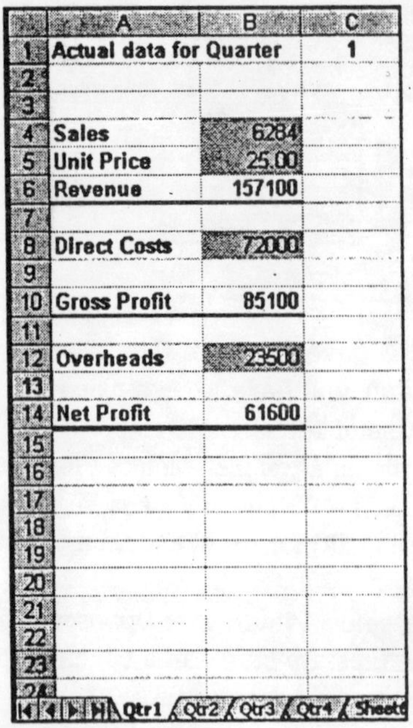

To minimise the work required for the actuals file, open BUDGET, copy columns A and B to a new worksheet, remove any existing data and shade the cells into which input is required. Figure 2.9 shows the first sheet of the actuals file. As this is a quarterly plan, four separate sets of actual data are required. Therefore the information in Figure 2.9 is copied into three further sheets and the sheets are named *Qtr 1*, *Qtr 2*, *Qtr 3* and *Qtr 4* respectively. To clarify which sheet is which a quarter number is entered into cell C1 of each sheet.

When creating the actuals file a decision will have to be made as to whether all the calculated data is entered or whether the spreadsheet will perform some of the calculations. For example, in Figure 2.9 this affects the revenue, gross profit and net profit. Having the spreadsheet calculate these figures can be a useful auditing technique as the results can be compared with the actual output if this has come from an accounting system or elsewhere.

Once completed this file should be saved and in this example the name ACTUALS has been used.

In the same way as the BUDGET file was converted to a template file, all the data should be removed from the ACTUALS file in order that this can also be saved as a template. It is suggested that the name ACTEMP be used.

PREPARING THE VARIANCE REPORT

In order to offer the user some degree of flexibility a variance report template can be created that allows a quarter to be selected and a variance report of the budget values versus the actual figures for that quarter to be produced.

The VARIANCE file will use file links to the ACTUALS and the BUDGET files. To make testing the spreadsheet simpler, open the BUDGET and ACTUALS files and ensure that some data, such as the test data shown in Figures 2.4 and 2.9, is entered.

To create the variance report template the line descriptions from the BUDGET file are required. Therefore copy column A from BUDGET and change the main title and the column headings as shown in Figure 2.10. Save this file as VARIANCE . Note that it is not necessary to save this file as .XLT or WKT template file as no variable data is required.

In order to produce a variance report for a specified quarter the user needs to be able to enter a quarter number into cell D1; then, using this information, the appropriate data from the appropriate file is picked up by the formulae in columns B and C. A simple subtraction of the actual from the budget is then required in column D.

Figure 2.10 Headings for variance report

	A	B	C	D
1	Variance report for Quarter			
2				
3		Budget	Actual	Variance
4	Sales			
5	Unit Price			
6	Revenue			
7				
8	Direct Costs			
9				
10	Gross Profit			
11				
12	Overheads			
13				
14	Net Profit			
15				

Assuming that a quarter number is entered into cell D1, a test is required to look at the contents of cell D1 and then pick up the appropriate date from the budget file.

The IF function is a logical function that considers a proposition and takes two different courses of action depending on whether the proposition is true or false. The format of this function is:

IF(proposition,true,false)

For example, entering the following formula into, say, cell B1:

IF(A1=6,A1*2,A1*3)

would be interpreted as: if the content of cell A1 is equal to 6 then multiply this by 2 and return the answer in B1, but if the content of cell A1 is not equal to 6 then multiply the content of cell A1 by 3 and return the answer in cell B1.

In addition to testing to see if a cell is equal to a given proposition the full range of logical operators can be used. These are:

=	equal to
>	greater than
>=	greater than or equal to
<	less than
<=	less than or equal to
<>	not equal to

Sometimes it is necessary to nest an IF function within another IF function, and this is required in cell B4 of the current example in order to pick up the appropriate data from the BUDGET file. The following formula is required.

In Excel

```
=IF($D$1=1,[Budget.xls]Budgets!B4,IF($D$1=2,[Budget.xls]Budgets!C4,
   IF($D$1=3,[Budget.xls]Budgets!D4,IF($D$1=4,[Budget.xls]Budgets!
      E4,"!!!"))))
```

In 1–2–3

```
@IF($D$1=1,<<Budget.WK4>>Budgets:B4..Budgets:B4,@IF($D$1=2,
   <<Budget.WK4>>Budgets:C4..Budgets:C4,@IF($D$1=3,
      <<Budget.WK4>>Budgets:D4..Budgets:D4,@IF($D$1=4,
         <<Budget.WK4>>Budgets:E4..Budgets:E4,"!!!"))))
```

This formula can be copied to the remaining cells in the budget column of the variance report. In order to ensure that a number between 1 and 4 is entered the above formula will return '!!!' in the cell if anything other than 1, 2, 3 or 4 is entered.

The above statement can be interpreted in the following way:

If the content of cell D1 is equal to 1 then the result will be the content of cell B4 from the *Budget* sheet of the BUDGET file. If this is not true then look to see if the content of cell D1 is equal to 2, and if it is the result will be the content of cell C4 from the *Budget* sheet of the BUDGET file. If this is not true then look to see if the content of cell D1 is equal to 3, and if it is the result will be the content of cell D4 from the *Budget* sheet of the BUDGET file. If this is not true then look to see if the content of cell D1 is equal to 4, and if it is the result will be the content of cell E4 from the *Budget* sheet of the BUDGET file. If this is not true then an invalid entry has been made in cell D1 and the result will be '!!!'.

As a reminder to the user to enter a valid entry into cell D1 the following IF function has also been entered into cell E1.

In Excel

```
=IF(OR(D1<1,D1>4),"Enter a quarter number between 1 and 4","")
```

In 1–2–3

```
@IF(((D1<1)#OR#(D1>4)),"Enter a quarter number between 1 and 4","")
```

Notice that in the above example the OR condition has been included in the IF statement. This in effect allows two or more propositions to be considered and, providing at least one is true, the true result of the IF function will be returned and only if all propositions are false will the false result of the function be returned.

In the above formula there are two propositions which look to see if the content of cell D1 is less than 1 OR the content or D1 is greater than 4. If either of these propositions is true the text 'Enter a quarter number between 1 and 4' will be returned, but if both propositions are false the cell will be left blank.

Because the BUDGET file is open, entering a number into cell D1 should return the budget data for that quarter. Figure 2.11 shows the variance report at this stage having entered 2 into cell D1.

A formula similar to that used for the budgets is required for the actual column of the variance report, but with a reference to the appropriate sheet of the ACTUALS file. The formula required in cell C4 is therefore as follows.

In Excel

```
=IF($D$1=1,[Actuals.xls]Qtr1!B4,IF($D$1=2,[Actuals.xls]Qtr2!B4,IF($D$1=3,
    [Actuals.xls]Qtr3!B4,IF($D$1=4,[Actuals.xls]Qtr4!B4,"!!!"))))
```

In 1–2–3

```
@IF($D$1=1,<<Actuals.WK4>>Qtr1:B4..Qtr1:B4,@IF($D$1=2,
    <<Actuals.WK4>>Qtr2:B4..Qtr2:B4,@IF($D$1=3,<<Actuals.WK4>>
        Qtr3:B4..Qtr3:B4,@IF($D$1=4,<<Actuals.WK4>>
            Qtr4:B4..Qtr4:B4,"!!!"))))
```

Figure 2.11 BUDGET file links for second quarter

	A	B	C	D
1	Variance report for Quarter			2
2				
3		Budget	Actual	Variance
4	Sales	6313		
5	Unit Price	25.00		
6	Revenue	157813		
7				
8	Direct Costs	71016		
9				
10	Gross Profit	86797		
11				
12	Overheads	21210		
13				
14	Net Profit	65587		
15				
16				

This formula can be copied for the remaining cells in column C. Figure 2.12 shows how the VARIANCE file will look at this stage, assuming that test data has been entered into the second quarter of the ACTUALS file.

Figure 2.12: BUDGET and ACTUAL file links for second quarter

	A	B	C	D
1	Variance report for Quarter			2
2				
3		Budget	Actual	Variance
4	Sales	6313	6445	
5	Unit Price	25	25.00	
6	Revenue	157813	161125	
7				
8	Direct Costs	71016	75230	
9				
10	Gross Profit	86797	85895	
11				
12	Overheads	21210	23000	
13				
14	Net Profit	65587	62895	
15				

To complete the variance report the actual data is subtracted from the budget data and Figure 2.13 is a variance report for the second quarter.

Figure 2.13: Variance report for the second quarter

	A	B	C	D
1	Variance report for Quarter			2
2				
3		Budget	Actual	Variance
4	Sales	6313	6445	-133
5	Unit Price	25	25.00	0.00
6	Revenue	157813	161125	-3313
7				
8	Direct Costs	71016	75230	-4214
9				
10	Gross Profit	86797	85895	902
11				
12	Overheads	21210	23000	-1790
13				
14	Net Profit	65587	62895	2692
15				

Figure 2.14 shows the variance report if an invalid quarter number is entered into cell D1.

Figure 2.14: Variance report with invalid quarter number

	A	B	C	D	E	F	G	H
1	Variance report for Quarter			5	Enter a quarter number between 1 and 4			
2	*London*							
3		Budget	Actual	Variance				
4	Sales	!!!	!!!	#VALUE!				
5	Unit Price	!!!	!!!	#VALUE!				
6	Revenue	!!!	!!!	#VALUE!				
7								
8	Direct Costs	!!!	!!!	#VALUE!				
9								
10	Gross Profit	!!!	!!!	#VALUE!				
11								
12	Overheads	!!!	!!!	#VALUE!				
13								
14	Net Profit	!!!	!!!	#VALUE!				
15								

Because the variance report looks for data in two named files, namely BUDGET and ACTUALS, it will be necessary to change these filenames to the filenames that each department in the organisation uses for a particular period's budgets and actuals. In Excel this is achieved through the use of the **Edit Links** command, in which it is possible to change the source filenames. Therefore, the Techno-Toy Leeds factory might change the name from BUDGET to LEEDS BUDGET. In 1–2–3 the **Edit Links** command does not allow for this, and therefore the **Edit Find&Replace** command can be used to change the filenames referenced in the formulae.

PREPARING THE YEAR-TO-DATE REPORT

The variance report is designed to calculate the variance for any given quarter. However, it is also useful to have a year-to-date report that shows the cumulative variance for a specified number of quarters.

Figure 2.15 shows a year-to-date variance report for two quarters.

Figure 2.15 Year-to-date variance report for two quarters

	A	B	C	D	E	F	G	H	I
1	Year-to-date report for how many quarters?				2	No data for quarter		3	Actuals
2									
3		Budget	Actual	Variance					
4	Sales	16080	16600	-520					
5	Average Unit Price	37.59	39.80	-2					
6	Revenue	604515	660750	-56235					
7									
8	Direct Costs	241806	210000	31806					
9									
10	Gross Profit	362709	450750	-88041					
11									
12	Overheads	30150	27000	3150					
13									
14	Net Profit	332559	423750	-91191					
15									

This report shows the cumulative budget data and the cumulative actual data to produce a year-to-date variance for the number of quarters that are specified in cell E1. As the actual data is added to the file only when it becomes available, cell H1 reports the first quarter for which there is no data. Therefore, with the above example it is only possible to prepare a year-to-date report for the first or second quarters, as there is not yet any data available for the third quarter.

To create the year-to-date file open the VARIANCE file, delete the range B4 to C14 and change the headings and column widths as shown in Figure 2.15.

A formula is required in cell H1 that will return the first quarter number in which there is no actual data. If there is data in all four quarters the cell will remain blank. This is achieved through the use of the "" at the end of the formula.

In Excel

```
=IF([Actuals.xls]Qtr1!$B$4=0,1,IF([Actuals.xls]Qtr2!$B$4=0,2,
    IF([Actuals.xls]Qtr3!$B$4=0,3,IF([Actuals.xls]Qtr4!$B$4=0,4,""))))
```

In 1–2–3

```
@IF(<<actuals.wk4>>$Qtr1:$B$4..$Qtr1:$B$4=0,1,
    @IF(<<actuals.wk4>>$Qtr2:$B$4..$Qtr2:$B$4=0,2,
        @IF(<<actuals.wk4>>$Qtr3:$B$4..$Qtr3:$B$4=0,3,
            @IF(<<actuals.wk4>>$Qtr4:$B$4..$Qtr4:$B$4=0,4,""))))
```

The following formula is required in cell B4 to produce the year-to-date budget amount based on the number of quarters entered into cell E1.

In Excel

```
=IF($E$1=1,[Budget.xls]Budgets!B4,IF($E$1=2,SUM
    ([Budget.xls]Budgets!B4:C4),IF($E$1=3,SUM([Budget.xls]Budgets!
        B4:D4),IF($E$1=4,SUM([Budget.xls]Budgets!B4:E4),"!!!"))))
```

In 1–2–3

```
IF($E$1=1,<<Budget.WK4>>Budgets:B4..Budgets:B4,@IF($E$1=2,
    @SUM(<<Budget.WK4>>Budgets:B4..Budgets:C4),@IF($E$1=3,
        @SUM(<<Budget.WK4>>Budgets:B4..Budgets:D4),@IF($E$1=4,
            @SUM(<<Budget.WK4>>Budgets:B4..Budgets:E4),"!!!"))))
```

If a number other than 1, 2, 3 or 4 is entered into cell E1 the above formula will return '!!!', alerting the user to the fact that a valid quarter number has not been entered. This formula can be copied to the remaining cells in the budget column, with the exception of the unit price. It is not appropriate to accumulate a unit price and therefore the average unit price is calculated in cell B5 by dividing the revenue by the sales.

A formula similar to that used to calculate the year-to-date budgets is required for the actuals as shown below.

In Excel

```
=IF($E$1>=$H$1,"No data",IF($E$1=1,[Actuals.xls]Qtr1!B4,
    IF($E$1=2,SUM([Actuals.xls]Qtr1:Qtr2!B4:B4),IF($E$1=3,
        SUM([Actuals.xls]Qtr1:Qtr4!B4:B4),IF($E$1=4,
            SUM([Actuals.xls]Qtr1:Qtr4!B4:B4),"!!!")))))
```

In 1–2–3

```
@IF($E$1>=$H$1,"No data",@IF($E$1=1,<<Actuals.WK4>>
    Qtr1:B5..Qtr1:B5,@IF($E$1=2,@SUM(<<Actuals.WK4>>
        Qtr1:B5..Qtr2:B5),@IF($E$1=3,@SUM(<<Actuals.WK4>>
            Qtr1:B5..Qtr3:B5),@IF($E$1=4,@SUM(<<Actuals.WK4>>
                Qtr1:B5..Qtr4:B5),"!!!")))))
```

The first part of the above formula compares the number of quarters entered into cell E1 with cell H1 which is reporting the actuals quarter there is no data. If E1 is greater than or equal to H1 the message 'No data' is returned, otherwise the appropriate number of periods are accumulated. As with the budget column the formula can be copied to the remaining cells, but again the unit price is changed to be the average unit price by dividing the revenue by the sales.

The year-to-date variance is calculated in the same way as in the variance report by subtracting the year-to-date actuals from the year-to-date budgets. An enhancement is made to this formula to check the contents of actuals in order that the variance will be left blank if the 'No data' message is returned for the actual. Therefore, the following formula is entered in cell D4 and copied for the remaining cells in the variance column.

In Excel

=IF(C4="No data","",B4-C4)

In 1–2–3

@IF(C4="No data","",B4-C4)

Figure 2.16 shows the year-to-date report when a quarter number for which there is no actual data is entered.

Figure 2.16 Year-to-date report with an invalid quarter number

	A	B	C	D	E	F	G	H	I
1	Year-to-date report for how many quarters?				3	No data for quarter		3	Actuals
2									
3		Budget	Actual	Variance					
4	Sales	18938	No data						
5	Average Unit Price	25.00	No data						
6	Revenue	473453	No data						
7									
8	Direct Costs	213054	No data						
9									
10	Gross Profit	260399	No data						
11									
12	Overheads	63632	No data						
13									
14	Net Profit	196767	No data						
15									

SUMMARY

The four files that have been developed in this chapter describe a method for producing a flexible budgetary control system. The flexibility is primarily due to the use of separate files for each module of the system, which means that different people can work on different parts of the system at the same time and users can choose to produce reports using selected data.

Before using the system it is important to ensure that all the files are in the same directory and that the links are referencing the correct files. It might be necessary to select **Edit Links** and amend the path if the system is installed on another user's computer. File links are an important feature of the spreadsheet, but if large numbers of files are referenced in this way, they can become difficult to manage. Other methods of referencing data across files are considered in the next chapter.

Chapter 3

Consolidating Data

INTRODUCTION

The budgetary control system described in Chapter 2 was for a single division or department. In many organisations it is necessary to consolidate, summate or aggregate the data from separate divisions to produce a divisional or corporate report.

The budgetary control system developed in the previous chapter has been distributed to the Bristol and Leeds factories and the budget and actual templates have been used by these factories to build their own systems. From this they can create their own variance reports.

AGGREGATING USING FILE LINKS

If there are only a small number of departments or divisions from which to aggregate data it is possible to create an aggregate file using straightforward file links.

Figure 3.1 is an aggregated budget report of the three Techno-Toy factories. This has been created by first opening the BUDGET template file and deleting the *Input* sheet completely, the unit price line completely, the four quarters formulae for the sales, direct costs and overheads. The following formula is then entered into cell B4.

In Excel

='[Budget London.xls]Budgets'!B4+'[Budget Bristol.xls]Budgets'!B4+'[Budget Leeds.xls]Budgets'!B4

The above formula assumes that the three regional budget files are called BUDGET LONDON, BUDGET BRISTOL and BUDGET LEEDS and that these files are stored in the same directory as the aggregated budget file. If a file is in a different directory then the full path to that directory must be stated.

Although this formula can be typed into the system, it is preferable, if possible, to open the files that are to be linked and to use the mouse to point to the cells that make up the formula.

This formula can be copied for the remainder of the Sales row and into the Revenue, Direct costs and Overheads rows.

In 1–2–3

```
+<<c:\budgets\budlond>>Budgets:B4..Budgets:B4+<< c:\budgets\
    budbrist>>Budgets:B4..Budgets:B4+<<c:\budgets\budleed>>
        Budgets:B4..Budgets:B4
```

In 1–2–3 it is necessary to enter the full path when linking cells across files and the mouse cannot be used to construct the formula. The above formula assumes the regional budget files have been called BUDLOND, BUDBRIST and BUDLEEDS and that they are all stored on the C drive in a directory called Budgets.

This formula can be copied for the remainder of the Sales row and into the Revenue, Direct costs and Overheads rows.

Figure 3.1 Aggregated budget file using file links

	A	B	C	D	E	F
1			Techno-Toy Ltd			
2		*Aggregate Budget for Leeds, Bristol and London, 19XX*				
3		Qtr1	Qtr2	Qtr3	Qtr4	Total
4	Sales	17040	17210	17383	17556	69189
5						
6	Revenue	426000	430260	434563	438908	1729731
7						
8	Direct Costs	167175	168847	170535	172241	678798
9						
10	Gross Profit	258825	261413	264027	266668	1050933
11						
12	Overheads	57500	58775	60098	61470	237843
13						
14	Net Profit	201325	202638	203930	205197	813090
15						

The aggregated file can be saved with the name AGGBUDGET. Every time AGGBUDGET is opened the system will ask whether the file links are to be updated. On answering 'yes' the formulae will be recalculated using the current values in the regional budget files. In other words, an up-to-date aggregated budget can be produced at any time.

Although file-linking is flexible from the point of view that when the source data is changed the dependent file containing the links is automatically updated, files containing many links can be slow to open and to recalculate. The construction of formulae with links to more than two or three files is also open to error, and there are other consolidation options available in the spreadsheet that might be more suitable.

OTHER CONSOLIDATION FEATURES

The consolidation features available in the spreadsheet allow for selected ranges of data from different files to be merged into a single file with options for summing, subtracting, averaging, etc.

To illustrate the consolidation features the variance report from the budgetary control system will be used. As the commands required to combine files and parts of files differ from spreadsheet to spreadsheet, the procedure for Excel and 1–2–3 is described separately.

Consolidating data with Excel

Excel provides a powerful set of consolidation tools through the **Data Consolidate** command. However, before using the command a set of files to be consolidated needs to be created. Using the templates created in Chapter 2, create a variance report for each of the three regional Techno-Toy factories and name these files VAR LONDON, VAR LEEDS and VAR BRISTOL. To simplify the consolidation procedure the range to be included in the consolidation in each file is named by selecting the range A3:D14, followed by **Insert Name Define**, calling the range Data_area.

Note that this would normally be done at the time of creating the variance template before distribution to the regional factories.

The next step is to create a new file that will form the consolidated report. Type an appropriate title for the report into cell A1 and then place the cursor on the cell that will be the top left cell of the consolidated range, which for this example will be B3.

Select **Data Consolidate**, which produces the dialogue box shown in

Figure 3.3. The default function for the consolidate command is Sum, i.e. the corresponding cells from the selected ranges will be summed. However, by clicking on the arrow to the right of the function box the other alternatives can be seen.

Figure 3.3 Excel Data Consolidate **dialogue box**

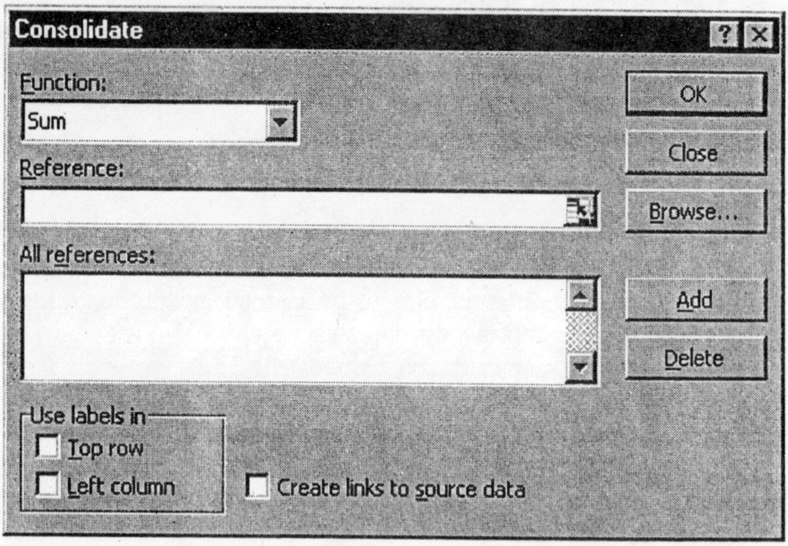

The reference box refers to the files or ranges that are to be consolidated. To complete this click on Browse and select the file VAR LONDON. After the exclamation mark (!) type the range name Data_area and then click Add which will display this reference in the All references box. Repeat this process for the files VAR LEEDS and VAR BRISTOL.

Check the Use labels in Top row and Left column boxes. This tells the system to assume that the top row and the left column of the specified range (Data_area) are labels. For this first example, also check the Create links to source data box. The dialogue box will now look like the one displayed in Figure 3.4.

On clicking OK the consolidation is performed and the spreadsheet appears as shown in Figure 3.5.

Figure 3.4 Completed Data Consolidate **dialogue box**

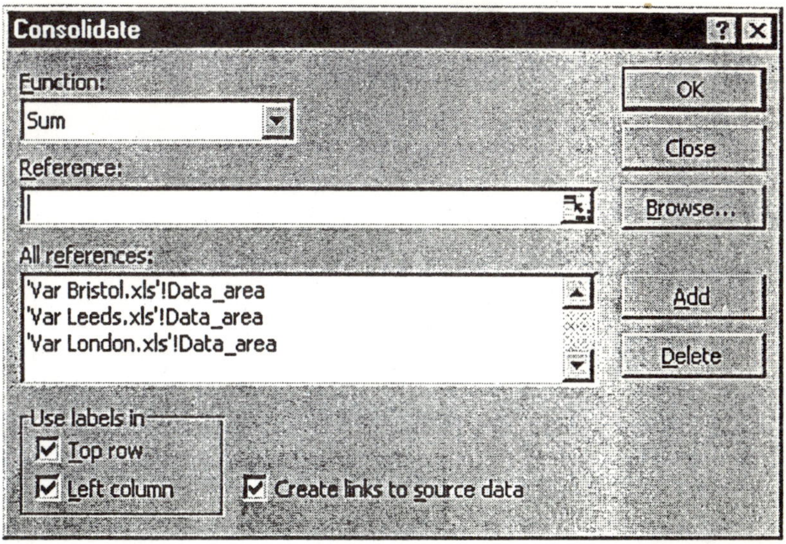

Figure 3.5 Aggregate variance report

	A	B	C	D	E	F	G
1	Aggregate Variance Report for the London, Leeds and Bristol						
2	Factories of Techno-Toy Ltd, 19XX						
3							
4				Budget	Actual	Variance	
8			Sales	17210	17340	-130	
12			Unit Price	75	75.00	0.00	
16			Revenue	430260	433500	-3240	
20			Direct Cos	168847	172230	-3383	
24			Gross Prof	261413	261270	143	
28			Overheads	58775	60600	-1825	
32			Net Profit	202638	200670	1968	
33							

To the left of the spreadsheet there are a series of plus signs. Clicking on the 2 at the top left of the screen will cause the source data that is used to produce the aggregated results to be displayed. This is shown in Figure 3.6.

Figure 3.6 Aggregate variance report with source data

	A	B	C	D	E	F	G
1	Aggregate Variance Report for the London, Leeds and Bristol						
2	Factories of Techno-Toy Ltd, 19XX						
3							
4				Budget	Actual	Variance	
5			Var Bristol	4949	4995	-46	
6			Var Leeds	5949	5900	49	
7			Var London	6313	6445	-133	
8		Sales		17210	17340	-130	
9			Var Bristol	25	25.00	0.00	
10			Var Leeds	25	25.00	0.00	
11			Var London	25	25.00	0.00	
12		Unit Price		75	75.00	0.00	
13			Var Bristol	123725	124875	-1150	
14			Var Leeds	148723	147500	1223	
15			Var London	157813	161125	-3313	
16		Revenue		430260	433500	-3240	
17			Var Bristol	45778	46000	-222	
18			Var Leeds	52053	51000	1053	
19			Var London	71016	75230	-4214	
20		Direct Costs		168847	172230	-3383	
21			Var Bristol	77947	78875	-928	
22			Var Leeds	96670	96500	170	
23			Var London	86797	85895	902	
24		Gross Profit		261413	261270	143	

This data is available because the Create links to source data box was checked in the **Data Consolidate** dialogue box.

In order to make the consolidation of a large number of data ranges a simple process, it is possible to use wildcard characters in the **Data Consolidate** dialogue box. The two most useful wildcard characters are the question mark (?), which is used to replace any single character in a filename or range name, and the asterisk (*), which is used to replace any number of characters at the end of the filename or range name.

Therefore, taking the above example, the **Data Consolidate** dialogue box could be completed as shown in Figure 3.7.

Figure 3.7 Data Consolidate **dialogue box using wildcards**

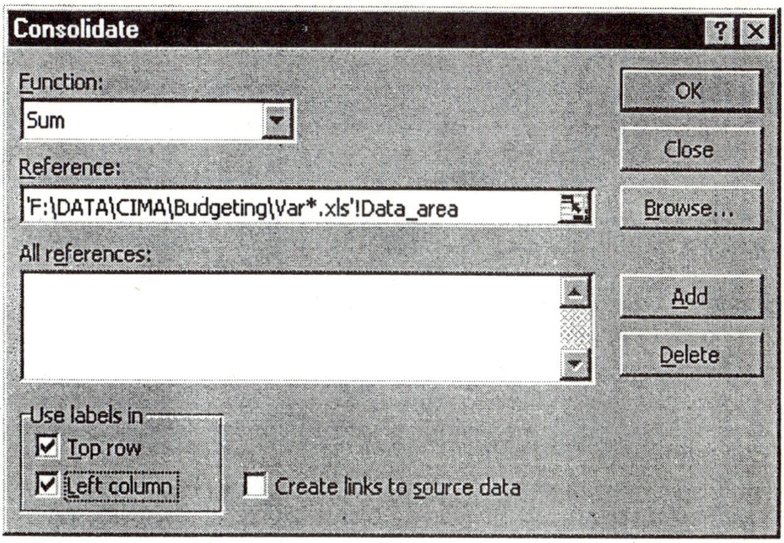

For this technique to work, previous thought has to be given to naming conventions of files and ranges, but it means that only one instruction has to be given before clicking OK to perform the consolidation as before.

In Figure 3.7 the Create link to source data box has not been checked. Figure 3.8 shows the results. Notice that the plus signs are not displayed on the left of the screen and it is not possible to view the source data. Although this means it is not possible to audit the files included in the consolidation, it does make the consolidated file smaller, and with a large number of files the operation will be much quicker.

Figure 3.8 Consolidation results without links to source files

	A	B	C	D	E	F
1	**Aggregate Variance Report for the London, Leeds and Bristol**					
2	**Factories of Techno-Toy Ltd, 19XX**					
3						
4			Budget	Actual	Variance	
5		Sales	17210	17340	-130	
6		Unit Price	75	75.00	0.00	
7		Revenue	430260	433500	-3240	
8		Direct Costs	168847	172230	-3383	
9		Gross Profit	261413	261270	143	
10		Overheads	58775	60600	-1825	
11		Net Profit	202638	200670	1968	
12						

Consolidating data with 1–2–3

Cells from different files can be added together in 1–2–3 through the **File Open Combine** command. However, before using the command a set of files to be consolidated need to be created. Using the templates created in Chapter 2 create a variance report for each of the three regional Techno-Toy factories and name these files VARLOND, VARLEEDS and VARBRIST. To simplify the consolidation procedure the range to be included in the consolidation is named in each of these three files by highlighting the range B4:D14, and then selecting **Range Name** and calling the range Data_area. It is important that only the data is included in the name and not the row or column headings.

The next step is to create a template that will form the basis of the consolidated report. This file needs to have the column and row headings that correspond with the data that will be consolidated. The quick way to produce this template is to once again open a VARIANCE file and then delete all the data and formulae, leaving only the headings in place. This file, which has been saved as CONSOL, is shown in Figure 3.9.

Figure 3.9 Template for consolidated report

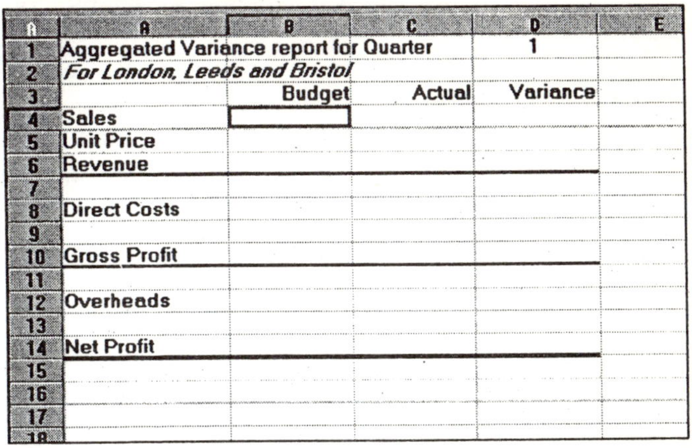

The cursor must be positioned on the cell that corresponds with the top left cell of the range to be consolidated. Therefore, for this example place the cursor on cell B4.

The first file to be included in the consolidation can now be added to the template with the command **File Open**, select the file VARLOND and then click on **Combine** which produces the dialogue box shown in Figure 3.10.

Figure 3.10 File combine dialogue box

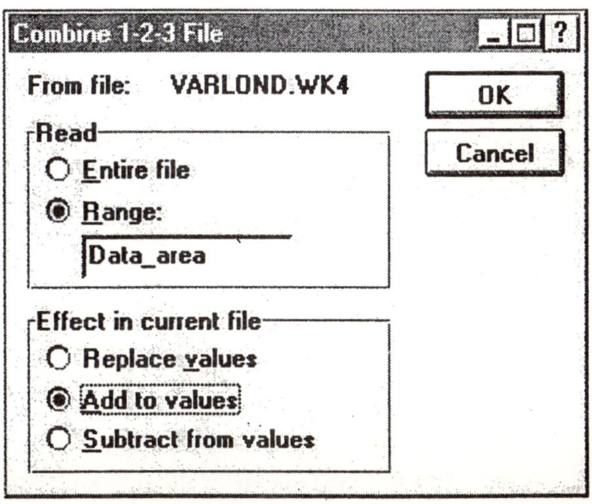

In this example it is the range named Data_area that is to be added and so this is entered in the range box. It is important to check the Add to values box before clicking on OK.

This procedure is repeated for the other two regional files, VARBRIST and VARLEEDS.

The range Data_area included the unit price, which has therefore also been added together. After adding in the file VARLEEDS the unit price should be changed to the average unit price by dividing the Revenue by the Sales. Figure 3.11 shows the resulting consolidated report.

Figure 3.11 Completed consolidated report

	A	B	C	D
1	Aggregated Variance report for Quarter			1
2	*For London, Leeds and Bristol*			
3		Budget	Actual	Variance
4	Sales	18790	19000	-210
5	Unit Price	30	30	0.00
6	Revenue	569750	576250	-6500
7				
8	Direct Costs	216863	226000	-9138
9				
10	Gross Profit	352888	350250	2638
11				
12	Overheads	51500	48300	3200
13				
14	Net Profit	301388	301950	-563
15				

SUMMARY

The file-linking features of the spreadsheet are a useful and flexible way of integrating data from a number of different files. However, if there are many files to be referenced in this way the resulting spreadsheet can become difficult to manage. It is therefore important to choose the most appropriate way of aggregating data. The Excel **Data Consolidate** command and the 1–2–3 **File Combine** command provide an alternative means of adding data together from different files without the need for linking files.

The examples shown in this chapter can be further automated through the use of macros in order that, especially in 1–2–3, the user does not have to enter the information for each file to be included in the consolidated report.

Chapter 4

Working With Spreadsheets

Having developed a budgetary control system such as the one shown in Chapter 2, different parts of the system can be used for different analysis and reporting purposes. In this chapter are explained some of the more useful commands and functions.

'WHAT-IF' ANALYSIS

'What-if' analysis is the process of changing assumptions in a plan in order to see the effect of the changes on the objectives. It is a direct product of the fact that, once a plan has been entered into the computer, it can be recalculated again and again at electronic speeds. Thus it is possible to change input data or input relationships and immediately recalculate the worksheet to see the impact of these changes on critical output factors.

A typical 'What-if' type of question might be to ask what effect a 2 per cent increase in direct costs will have on the net profit, or what effect will a further 30-day delay in receiving cash from the debtors have on the overdraft and/or return on investment.

'What-if' questions may be put one at a time, or several applied at once. If it is necessary to investigate the effect of two simultaneous changes in the assumptions it is usually advantageous to also consider these one at a time, so that the individual effects as well as the joint effects are known. Irrespective of whether single or multiple changes to input are made, multiple output will usually be monitored.

The spreadsheet provides for several different levels of 'What-if' analysis. In the simplest case, all that is required is to change the value of a data cell and the impact of the change will be seen as soon as the worksheet is recalculated. For more powerful 'What-if' there are *data* or *'What-if'* tables, which allow a series of 'What-if' questions to be analysed at one time, producing a tabular report of the possible results.

SIMPLE 'WHAT-IF' ANALYSIS

For even the simplest 'What-if' analysis to be successful it is necessary for a plan to have been carefully constructed with correct relationships and logic.

The benefits of using data input forms can be seen when it comes to performing 'What-if' analysis. Figure 4.1 shows the effect of changing the sales growth rate in the budget file used in Chapter 2. To increase the growth rate to 1.5 per cent required only a single cell (C5 on the *Input* sheet) to be changed, and every other cell that has a direct or indirect relationship to this cell will be recalculated.

Figure 4.1 Results of simple 'What-if' analysis on sales volume

	A	B	C	D	E	F
1			Techno-Toy London Ltd			
2			*Summary Budget for 19XX*			
3		Qtr1	Qtr2	Qtr3	Qtr4	Total
4	Sales	6250	6344	6439	6535	25568
5	Unit Price	25.00	25.00	25.00	25.00	
6	Revenue	**156250**	**158594**	**160973**	**163387**	**639204**
7						
8	Direct Costs	70313	71367	72438	73524	287642
9						
10	Gross Profit	**85938**	**87227**	**88535**	**89863**	**351562**
11						
12	Overheads	21000	21210	21422	21636	85268
13						
14	Net Profit	**64938**	**66017**	**67113**	**68227**	**266294**
15						

DATA TABLES FOR 'WHAT-IF' ANALYSIS

Regardless of whether it is the opening values or the growth factors that require analysis, if a large number of changes are required in order to establish the most sensitive variable, or the most appropriate value, the individual changing of the data can be a lengthy process.

Both Excel and 1–2–3 provide a feature whereby a range of data for a particular input variable or variables can be entered into a separate part of the worksheet, and this data can then be compared against one or more output variables in the plan. For example, in order to ascertain the most profitable volume level, a range of different opening volumes can be entered into the worksheet and the effect of each of these can be seen on net profit. The command used to perform this type of analysis is **Data Table** in Excel and **Range Analysis What-if** in 1–2–3.

There are two types of data table in Excel: a one-way and a two-way table. 1–2–3 also has the option for a three-way 'What-if' table.

A one-way table allows one input factor to be analysed against as many output variables as required. With a two-way table there are two input factors, and a single output variable.

One-way data tables

A one-way data table can be created to look at varying opening volumes for the BUDGET file of Techno-Toy Ltd. For this example the table will be placed on the *Input* sheet.

The first step is to decide on the volume values that are to be used as 'What-if' data. The current volume value in the budget file is 6,250 and so, for this example, values from 6,000 to 7,000 increasing in steps of 100 will be used. There are several ways to enter a series of values into the spreadsheet. One of the quicker ways is to enter the first two values and then to select both cells and drag the cross-hair marker from the bottom right of the highlighted range for the number of cells required.

The next step is to decide the cells in the main model on which the effect of the 'What-if' is to be performed. In this case it is the net profit for the second and fourth quarters and the total net profit. Therefore, references to these cells need to be made at the table area. Figure 4.2 shows the table construction to this stage. Note that the position of the output references in row 12 in relation to the input cells in column B is important.

To calculate the table in Figure 4.2, select the range B12:E23 and then select **Data Table** in Excel or **Range Analysis What-if** in 1–2–3. Figures 4.3 and 4.4 show the resulting dialogue boxes for both systems.

Figure 4.2 Preparation for a one-way data or 'What-if' table

	A	B	C	D	E
1	**Budget input form**				
2					
3		**Opening**	**Growth**	**Opening**	
4		**Value**	**Rate**	**Proportion**	
5	**Sales**	6250	1.00%		
6	**Unit Price**	25	0.00%		
7					
8	**Direct Costs**			45.00%	of turnover
9	**Overhead Costs**	21000	1.00%		
10					
11			**Qtr 2**	**Qtr 4**	**Total**
12			65587	66905	263672
13		6000			
14		6100			
15		6200			
16	**V**	6300			
17	**o**	6400			
18	**l**	6500			
19	**u**	6600			
20	**m**	6700			
21	**e**	6800			
22		6900			
23		7000			
24					

Budgets | **Input** | Sheet3 | Sheet4 | Sheet5 | Sheet6 | Sheet7

Figure 4.3 Data Table **dialogue box in Excel**

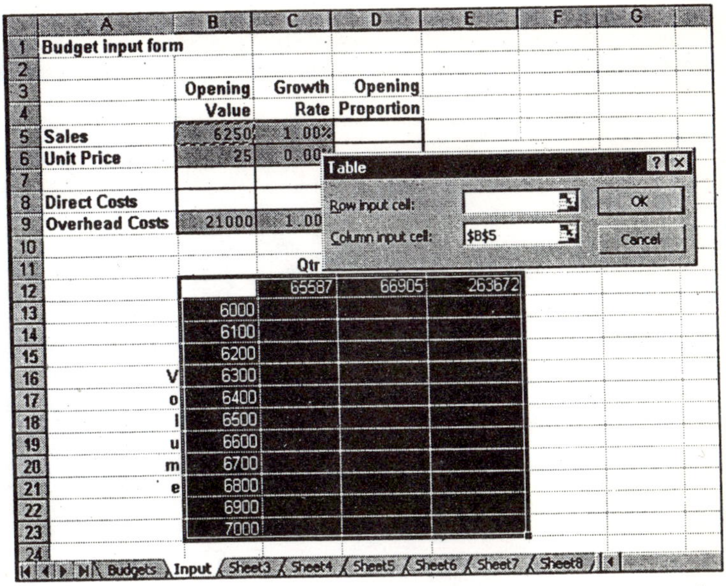

As this is a one-way table only one input cell is required. In this example the sales volume is the input variable, and therefore a reference to cell B5 is required in the Column input cell box.

Figure 4.4 Data Table **dialogue box in 1–2–3**

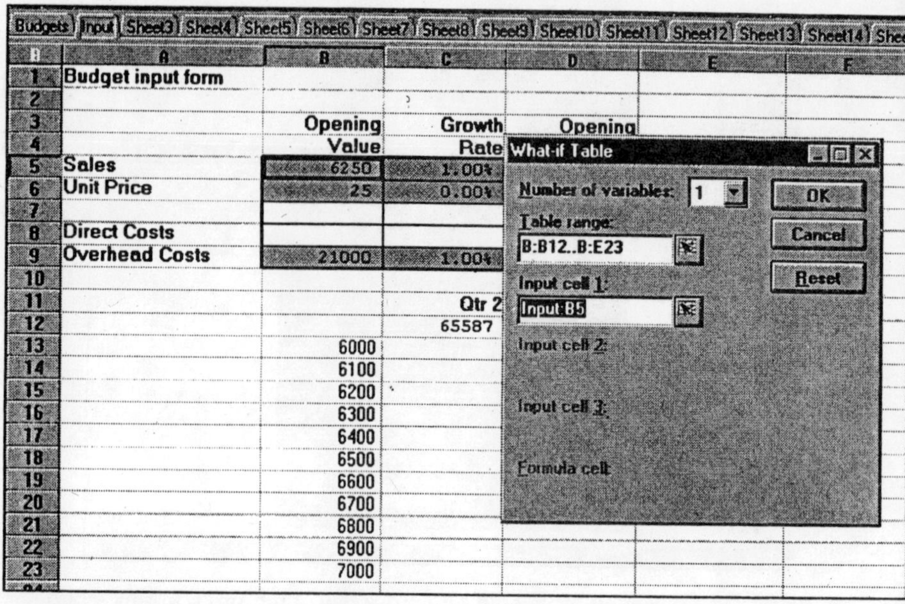

As this is a one-way 'What-if' table in 1–2–3 it is necessary to select 1 in the number of variables box and then to select cell B5 for the Input cell 1 box.

On clicking OK the table is calculated and the results, which are the same in both Excel and 1–2–3, are displayed, as shown in Figure 4.5.

Figure 4.5 Calculated one-way data table

	A	B	C	D	E
1	**Budget input form**				
2					
3		**Opening**	**Growth**	**Opening**	
4		**Value**	**Rate**	**Proportion**	
5	**Sales**	6250	1.00%		
6	**Unit Price**	25	0.00%		
7					
8	**Direct Costs**			45.00%	of turnover
9	**Overhead Costs**	21000	1.00%		
10					
11			**Qtr 2**	**Qtr 4**	**Total**
12			65587	66905	263672
13		6000	62115	63364	249715
14		6100	63504	64780	255298
15		6200	64893	66197	260881
16	**V**	6300	66281	67614	266464
17	**o**	6400	67670	69030	272047
18	**l**	6500	69059	70447	277630
19	**u**	6600	70448	71863	283213
20	**m**	6700	71836	73280	288796
21	**e**	6800	73225	74697	294379
22		6900	74614	76113	299962
23		7000	76003	77530	305545
24					

Budgets | **Input** | Sheet3 | Sheet4 | Sheet5 | Sheet6 | Sheet7

What has actually happened during the calculation process is that the first value in the input range (6,000) is entered into the specified input cell (B5). The worksheet is recalculated and the resulting net profit values are placed in cells C13, D13 and E13. The next input value (6,100) is then entered into cell B5, the worksheet is recalculated and the resulting net profit values are placed in cells C14, D14 and E14. This process is repeated for all the values in the input range. Only when all the calculation is complete is the table displayed.

From this table it can be seen, for example, that with an opening sales volume of 6,200 the total net profit at the end of the year would be £260,881. This takes into consideration all the other assumptions built into the model.

There is no limit to the number of output cells that can be included in a one-way table. The only point to watch is that there is a relationship between the input variable and the output cell. This is easily checked by manually making a change to an input variable and observing the cells in the model this change affects.

Differences between Excel and 1–2–3

There are some important differences in the way Excel and 1–2–3 calculate data tables. In Excel the command actually places a formula using the Table function into each of the cells in the table range. Therefore, if any changes are made to data in the main plan, or to the input or output ranges, the table will automatically be recalculated to reflect the changes. This also means that there can be multiple data tables on a spreadsheet and all can be kept up to date simultaneously. In fact, when working with very large tables, or many tables, the recalculation time can sometimes become unacceptable. Therefore, there is an option in **Tools Options Calculations** to set recalculation to 'Automatic except Tables', which means that it will be necessary to press F9 to recalculate the data tables.

In 1–2–3 the command leaves absolute values as the results in the table and thus, if changes are made to the main plan or to the input or output data, it is necessary to re-evaluate the table. If there is only one 'What-if' table on the spreadsheet this can be quickly achieved by pressing the F8 Table function key. However, this will recalculate only the *active* table, or the last one to be evaluated. Therefore, if there are multiple tables on a spreadsheet they must be individually re-evaluated when changes are made.

A disadvantage of data tables in Excel is the fact that they must be located on the same worksheet as the input data, which effectively means that it is not possible to have a separate sheet on which all the data tables for an application are placed. This is not a problem in 1–2–3 as tables can be located on separate sheets. Therefore, in the above example, the table does not have to be on the *Input* sheet in 1–2–3, but it does in Excel.

Two-way data tables

The previous examples showed the effect of changing a single variable, i.e. the opening sales value of the BUDGET file. A two-way table can be created to see the combined effect of changing both the sales volume and the unit price. For this example the same sales volume figures will be used as for the one-way table, and unit price values of £20 to £40, increasing by £5, will be used. With a two-way table it is only possible to have one output cell. Therefore, in this example, the effects of changing the sales volume and the unit price will be tested against the year-end total net profit.

Figures 4.6 and 4.7 show the outline of the two-way table together with the completed table dialogue boxes for Excel and 1–2–3.

Figure 4.6 Preparation of a two-way data table in Excel

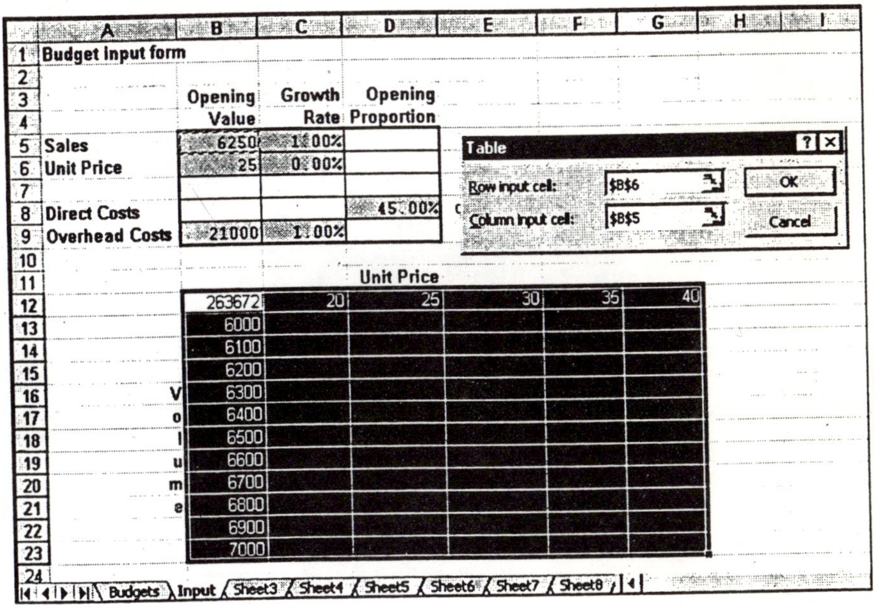

It is important to place the reference to the output cell in the correct place for this table to calculate correctly. In both Figure 4.6 and Figure 4.7 a reference to cell F14 of the *Budget* sheet has been made in cell B12.

Figure 4.7 Preparation of a two-way 'What-if' table in 1–2–3

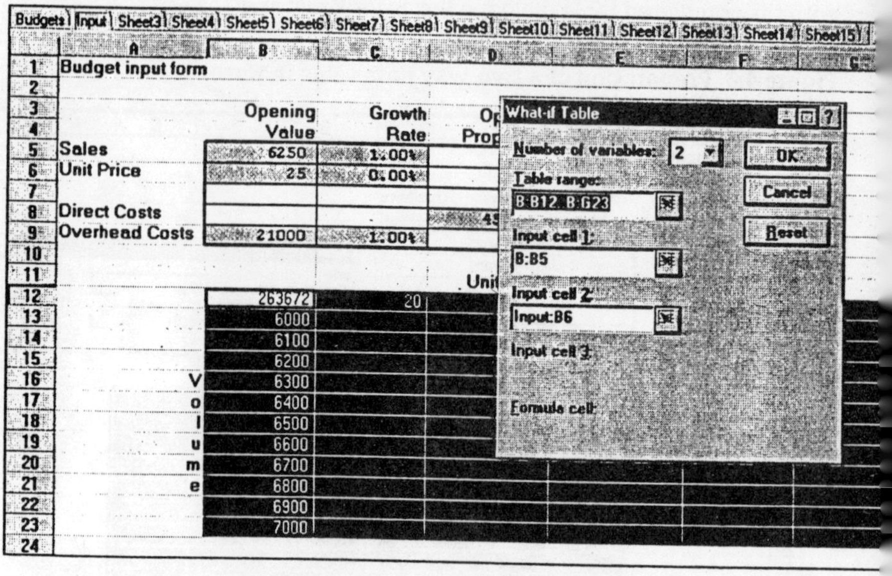

In 1–2–3, as can be seen in Figure 4.7, it is necessary to specify that there are two input variables. When specifying the cell references for the input variable it is important to reference the vertical variable in the table first. In this example, it is the sales volume in cell B5.

Figure 4.8 shows the results of the two-way table.

Figure 4.8 Completed two-way table

	A	B	C	D	E	F	G
1	**Budget input form**						
2							
3		**Opening**	**Growth**	**Opening**			
4		**Value**	**Rate**	**Proportion**			
5	**Sales**	6250	1.00%				
6	**Unit Price**	25	0.00%				
7							
8	**Direct Costs**			45.00%	of turnover		
9	**Overhead Costs**	21000	1.00%				
10							
11				**Unit Price**			
12		263672	20	25	30	35	40
13		6000	182718	249715	316711	383708	450705
14		6100	187184	255298	323411	391524	459637
15		6200	191651	260881	330111	399340	468570
16	**V**	6300	196117	266464	336810	407157	477503
17	**o**	6400	200584	272047	343510	414973	486436
18	**l**	6500	205050	277630	350210	422789	495369
19	**u**	6600	209517	283213	356909	430606	504302
20	**m**	6700	213983	288796	363609	438422	513235
21	**e**	6800	218450	294379	370309	446238	522168
22		6900	222916	299962	377008	454054	531100
23		7000	227382	305545	383708	461871	540033
24							

Budgets | **Input** | Sheet3 | Sheet4 | Sheet5 | Sheet6 | Sheet7 | Sheet8

With a two-way table, on clicking OK in the **Data Table** dialogue box, the first value in the column input range (6,000) and the first value in the row input range (20) are entered into the specified input cells (B5 and B6 respectively). The worksheet is recalculated and the resulting total net profit value is placed in cell C13. The value 6,000 is then left in cell B5 and 25 is placed in B6. The worksheet is recalculated and the resulting total net profit is placed in cell D13. This process is repeated for all the cells in the input range.

From this table it can be seen, for example, that at a price of £20 and an opening sales volume of 6,200 the total net profit at the end of the year would be £191,651. This takes into consideration all the other assumptions made in the model.

CHOOSING THE RIGHT FUNCTIONS

There are so many built-in functions in spreadsheets today that it can be difficult to know which one to choose for which application. One area that often becomes unnecessarily complex is when it is necessary to incorporate lengthy IF statements into formulae.

The IF function is widely used, and indeed it was required in the budgetary control system that was developed in Chapter 2. However, sometimes there are other functions that can be used in place of IF. The example discussed here uses LOOKUP tables to test for ranges of data instead of nested IF functions. By way of an example it has been decided to consider paying a staff bonus at Techno-Toy Ltd, and the exact amount payable will be dependent on the gross profit. Figure 4.9 shows the budget file with a line inserted ready for the bonus calculation.

Figure 4.9 Budget file ready for bonus calculation

	A	B	C	D	E	F
1			Techno-Toy London Ltd			
2			*Summary Budget for 19XX*			
3		Qtr1	Qtr2	Qtr3	Qtr4	Total
4	Sales	6250	6313	6376	6439	25378
5	Unit Price	25.00	25.00	25.00	25.00	
6	**Revenue**	**156250**	**157813**	**159391**	**160985**	**634438**
7						
8	Direct Costs	70313	71016	71726	72443	285497
9						
10	**Gross Profit**	**85938**	**86797**	**87665**	**88541**	**348941**
11						
12	Bonus					
13	Overheads	21000	21210	21422	21636	85268
14						
15	**Net Profit**	**64938**	**65587**	**66243**	**66905**	**263672**
16						
17						
18						
19						
20						
21						
22						
23						

Budgets / Input / Sheet3 / Sheet4 / Sheet5 / Sheet6 / Sheet7 / Sheet8

It has been decided that bonus of 1 per cent of the gross profit will be paid if the gross profit is between £85,000 and £86,000; 2 per cent will be paid if the gross profit is between £86,001 and £88,000; and 3 per cent will be paid if the gross profit exceeds £88,000.

Using the IF function, the logic required for this calculation in cell B12 would be as follows.

In Excel

```
=B10*IF(B10<85000,0,IF(B10<86000,1%,IF(B10<88000,2%,3%)))
```

In 1–2–3

```
+B10*@IF(B10<85000,0,@IF(B10<86000,0.01,@IF(B10<88000,0.02,0.03)))
```

Following the design rules discussed in Chapter 2, it is not recommended to embed values into a formula because it makes the formula more difficult to edit and the values cannot be seen by the user. Therefore, when using an IF function such as this, the bonus values should be entered separately into the spreadsheet. Figure 4.10 shows how the bonus data has been entered into a small table, and then the above formula can be rewritten as follows.

In Excel

```
=B10*IF(B10<$B$20,$C$19,IF(B10<$B$21,$C$20,IF(B10<$B$22,$C$21,$C$22)))
```

In 1–2–3

```
+B10*@IF(B10<$B$20,$C$19,@IF(B10<$B$21,$C$20,@IF(B10<$B$22,$C$21,
   $C$22)))
```

To complete the updating of this plan it would be necessary to amend the formula for the net profit to take account of the bonus payments.

The effect of the last example above is to perform a range check inasmuch as a different bonus is required depending on the profit level. Nested IF function formulae can become quite long, and it is often difficult to get the syntax absolutely right, especially in terms of opening and closing parentheses. The VLOOKUP and HLOOKUP functions provide a much clearer method of working with ranges.

The format of the two functions is the same:

```
VLOOKUP([search value],[table range],[column offset])
HLOOKUP([search value],[table range],[row offset])
```

Figure 4.10 Bonus calculated with IF function and external references

	A	B	C	D	E	F
1		Techno-Toy London Ltd				
2		*Summary Budget for 19XX*				
3		Qtr1	Qtr2	Qtr3	Qtr4	Total
4	Sales	6250	6313	6376	6439	25378
5	Unit Price	25.00	25.00	25.00	25.00	
6	Revenue	156250	157813	159391	160985	634438
7						
8	Direct Costs	70313	71016	71726	72443	285497
9						
10	Gross Profit	85938	86797	87665	88541	348941
11						
12	Bonus	859	1736	1753	2656	
13	Overheads	21000	21210	21422	21636	85268
14						
15	Net Profit	64938	65587	66243	66905	263672
16						
17						
18		G. Profit	Bonus			
19		0	0%			
20		85000	1%			
21		86000	2%			
22		88000	3%			
23						
24						

Budgets / Input / Sheet3 / Sheet4 / Sheet5 / Sheet6 / Sheet7 / Sheet8

The VLOOKUP function begins by comparing the search value with the first column in the table range. If an exact match to the search value cannot be found the next lowest value is used. The result is then the contents of the cell in the same row, offset by the specified number of columns.

Consider the results of Figure 4.11.

Figure 4.11 Using the VLOOKUP function

	A	B	C	D	E
1					
2					
3		1000	1300	1500	900
4		1	1	2	0
5					
6		0	0		
7		1000	1		
8		1500	2		
9		2000	3		
10					

The formula in cell B4 is as follows.

In Excel

=VLOOKUP(B3,$B$6:$C$9,2)

In 1–2–3

@VLOOKUP(B3,$B$6..$C$9,1)

These are interpreted as:

look up the value in cell B3 (1,000) in the first column of the table range B6 to C9 and then return the value in the second column (1).

The reference to the table range must be absolute in order that it remains fixed when the formula is extrapolated to cells C3 to E3.

Looking at the formula in cell C3, the system is looking for the value 1,300 in the first column of the table range B6 to C9. This value is not there, so the VLOOKUP function will take the next lowest number, which is 1,000, and the value in the second column is returned (1).

For the VLOOKUP function to work in this way the values in the first column of the table must be sorted in ascending order.

Note that in 1–2–3 the first column of the table is seen as column 0 and thus if the second column is required for the result the last part of the function is 1 as opposed to 2 in Excel.

Using the VLOOKUP function to calculate the bonus required in cell B12 of the BUDGET file, the following formula is required.

In Excel

=B10*VLOOKUP(B10,$B$19:$C$22,2)

In 1–2–3

+B10*@VLOOKUP(B10,$B$19..$C$22,1)

In other words, the function is to look up the value in B10 (85,938) in the first column of the table range B19 to C22. If an exact match cannot be found then the next lowest value is used (85,000 in this case) and the value in the second column is the result of the function. Therefore the contents of cell B10 are multiplied by 1 per cent and that is the bonus payable.

The lookup table could have been oriented the other way with the search values (gross profit) across row 19 and the bonus percentages below in row 20, and then the HLOOKUP function would be used instead of VLOOKUP.

There is no limit to the number of columns in a VLOOKUP table or rows in a HLOOKUP table that can be incorporated. For example, in the above case it might be necessary to have different bonus values for the third and fourth quarters which could be entered as a third column in the table and the formula in cell D12 would then be as follows.

In Excel

=D10*VLOOKUP(D10,$B$19:$C$22,3)

In 1–2–3

+D10*@VLOOKUP(D10,$B$19..$C$22,2)

The LOOKUP functions are very useful spreadsheet tools, and the example shown here is only one application. It is strongly recommended that, having experimented with this example, readers take time to explore the application of LOOKUP functions in other areas.

SUMMARY

This chapter has looked at two important areas that should be explored when developing and working with spreadsheets. 'What-if' analysis is really what made spreadsheet technology so popular. Without the ability to change data and assumptions the spreadsheet would not be the powerful analytical tool it is seen to be.

As the spreadsheet has developed over the years the range of functions available has also increased considerably. It is difficult to know whether the best function for the job has been selected, and in this short book only one example of how one function can enable a less complex formula to be used has been shown.

▩ **Chapter 5**

Working with Other Applications

INTRODUCTION

Having prepared a budgetary control system in the spreadsheet, it is sometimes necessary to report on certain aspects of the system in management reports or other documentation. Alternatively, it might be useful to incorporate data or graphs in a presentation.

The flexibility of the Windows operating systems makes it possible to reference or copy data from one application in another application. The process can be either *static* or *dynamic.*

A static copying of data from one application to another means that there is no link between the copied data and the original source. Therefore, if any changes are made to the original data these will not be reflected in the copy. However, if a link is made at the time of copying the data a *dynamic* reference has been established and if the original data is changed an option to update the referenced data is provided.

To illustrate these features the aggregated variance report that was created in Chapter 3 will be placed in a Word document. Both static and dynamic options are described. Although the example shown here uses Microsoft Word the principle is the same with other Windows word processors.

USING SPREADSHEET DATA IN A WORD PROCESSOR

The **Edit Copy** command is used to copy data from the spreadsheet on to the Windows Clipboard and then the **Edit Paste** or **Edit Paste Special** command is used within the word processor.

For example, to copy the range A3 to D14 of the variance report for the London factory of Techno-Toy into a Word document the following is required.

First open the spreadsheet file, which in this case would be VAR LONDON in Excel or VARLOND in 1–2–3. Select the range to be copied and either click on the Copy icon on the toolbar or select **Edit Copy**. This places the selected range on the clipboard.

Go to the point in the Word document at which the spreadsheet range is to be placed.

Clicking on the Paste icon on the toolbar or selecting **Edit Paste** will copy the range into the document without any links. Figure 5.1 shows how the range from the variance report will appear in Word.

Figure 5.1 Copied spreadsheet range in a Word document

	Budget	Actual	Variance
Sales	8000	8100	−100
Unit Price	38	38	0.00
Revenue	300000	303750	-3750
Direct Costs	120000	130000	−10000
Gross Profit	180000	173750	6250
Overheads	15000	12000	3000
Net Profit	165000	161750	3250

The data in Word is seen as a table and there is no way of telling which spreadsheet this data came from. It will look exactly the same if it is copied from Excel or 1–2–3. If any of the information in this table requires changing this can be done directly in the document as this table is now just another part of the Word document.

Figure 5.1 shows exactly how the data appears in Word, and it may be necessary to reformat the table to better suit the document.

If **Edit Paste Special** is selected instead of **Edit Paste** the option to link the data to the spreadsheet file is given. Figure 5.2 shows the Word dialogue box after selecting **Edit Paste Special**.

Figure 5.2 Paste Special **dialogue box**

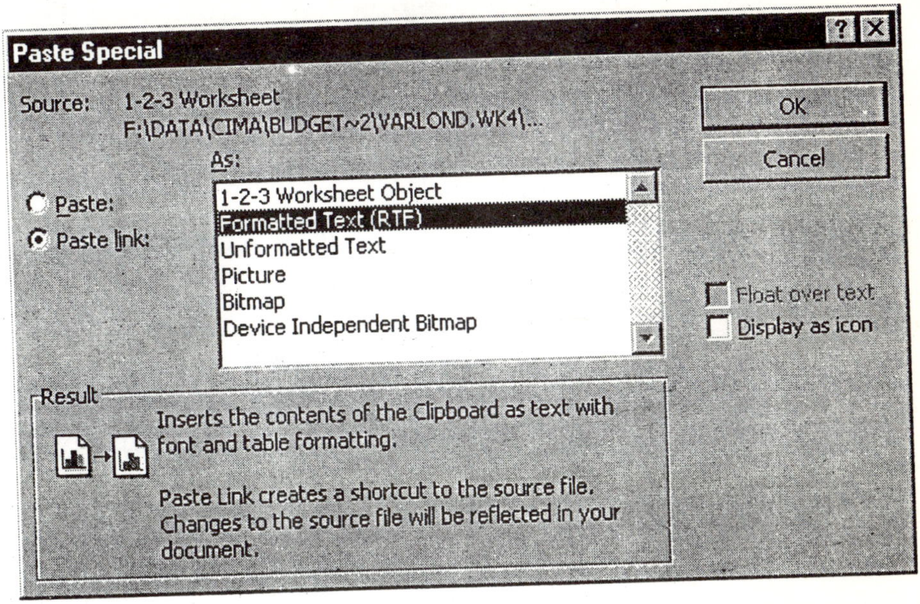

From Figure 5.2 it can be seen that Paste link has been selected. The source file is shown at the top of the dialogue box and in this example the 1–2–3 file has been used. The selected format for the incoming data is Formatted Text and the Result box at the bottom of the dialogue box explains how the selection format will be treated in Word. The results will appear to be the same as those shown in Figure 5.1. However, by placing the cursor over any of the cells in the table they will be shaded, which indicates that there is a file link. This is illustrated in Figure 5.3.

To test the file link, save and close the Word document. Go to the spreadsheet and change the quarter number in the variance file to report a different quarter. Save and close the variance report. Reopen the Word document and go to the spreadsheet extract that was linked, and notice that the data has changed to reflect what is currently in the variance report file.

This procedure is especially useful when regular management reports are required, in which little of the narrative changes on a periodic basis, but when up-to-date figures from the budgetary control system are required. However, there are occasions when it might not be appropriate to change the spreadsheet data in document when it is retrieved from disk. The **Edit**

Links command can be used to control how the links are managed. By default the links are updated automatically, but if this is changed to manual, a prompt to update links will be given when the document is opened. If it is decided that the links are no longer required they can be permanently broken through this dialogue box, which is shown in Figure 5.4.

Figure 5.3 Linked spreadsheet data showing highlighted cells

	Budget	Actual	Variance
Sales	7323	6445	878
Unit Price	25	25.00	0.00
Revenue	183063	161125	21938
Direct Costs	82378	75230	7148
Gross Profit	100684	85895	14789
Overheads	21210	23000	-1790
Net Profit	79474	62895	16579

Figure 5.4 Edit Links **dialogue box in Word**

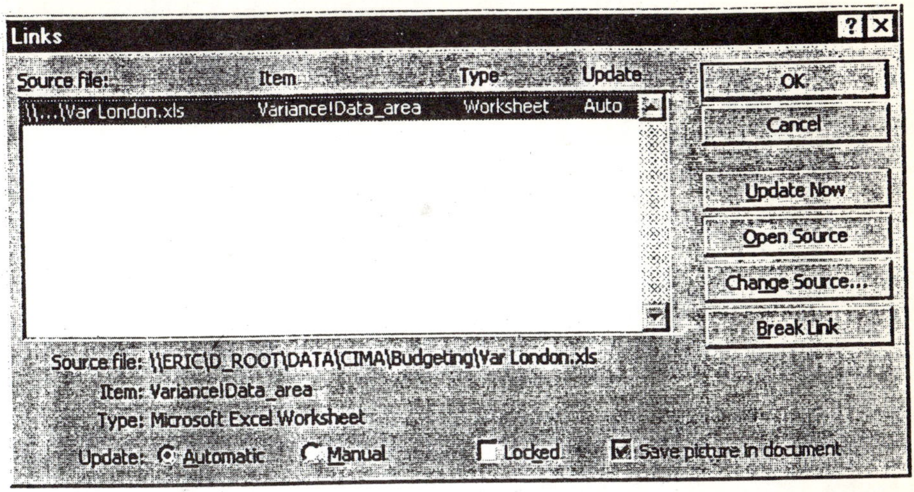

In both the above examples the data in the word processor can be directly edited as it is displayed as a Word table. Alternatively paste the spreadsheet, with or without links, as a worksheet object into the word processor.

Figure 5.5 Word Paste Special **dialogue box**

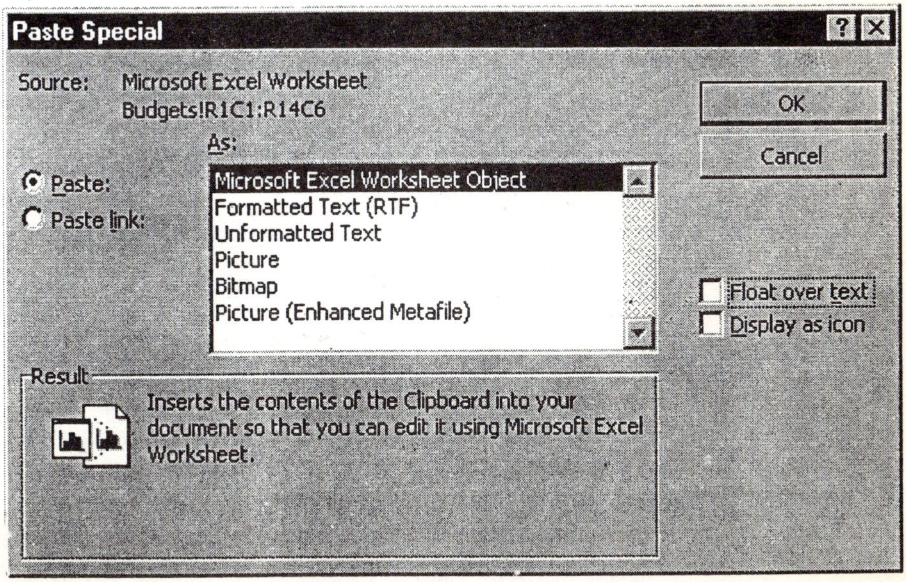

Figure 5.5 shows the **Paste Special** dialogue box in Word after copying the range A1 to F14 of the Excel BUDGET file for the London factory of Techno-Toy Ltd.

In this example no link has been specified, and Figure 5.6 shows the resulting display in Word.

Figure 5.6 Excel spreadsheet data as an object in the word processor

Techno-Toy London Ltd *Summary Budget for 19XX*					
	Qtr1	Qtr2	Qtr3	Qtr4	Total
Sales	7250	7323	7396	7470	29438
Unit Price	25.00	25.00	25.00	25.00	
Revenue	**181250**	**183063**	**184893**	**186742**	**735948**
Direct Costs	81563	82378	83202	84034	331176
Gross Profit	**99688**	**100684**	**101691**	**102708**	**404771**
Overheads	21000	21210	21422	21636	85268
Net Profit	**78688**	**79474**	**80269**	**81072**	**319503**

As can be seen in Figure 5.6 the data is not a table, and it has been resized to fit in the current margins. Placing the cursor somewhere on the object and clicking once displays the message 'Double-Click to Edit Microsoft Excel Object' at the bottom of the screen.

Double-clicking on the object will open Microsoft Excel with the spreadsheet data so that changes may be made.

If a link to the original spreadsheet file had been made then double-clicking would open the original file for editing purposes.

SUMMARY

The copy and paste techniques illustrated here can be applied in the same way with other Windows applications, and the option to link or not to link is available as well. In addition, the flexibility of Windows has been shown with the above examples in that spreadsheet data has been taken from Lotus 1–2–3 and has been linked within the Microsoft Word word processor. It has not mattered that applications from different software houses have been used.

However, it should be mentioned that this is not always the case and that, if frequent linking between applications is required, it is recommended that a common suite of application programs be used. If this is not possible it is important to ensure that the applications have been installed with the required file transfer utilities enabled.